MARITIME TRANSPORTATION SYSTEM SECURITY RECOMMENDATIONS

FOR

THE NATIONAL STRATEGY FOR MARITIME SECURITY

OCTOBER 2005

FOREWORD

By signing National Security Presidential Directive-41/Homeland Security Presidential Directive-13 (NSPD-41/HSPD-13) (Maritime Security Policy, December 21, 2004) President Bush underscored the importance of securing the Maritime Domain, which is defined as *"All areas and things of, on, under, relating to, adjacent to, or bordering on a sea, ocean, or other navigable waterway, including all maritime-related activities, infrastructure, people, cargo, and vessels and other conveyances."* NSPD-41/HSPD-13 established a Maritime Security Policy Coordinating Committee—the first coordinating committee tasked specifically to address this issue—to oversee the development of a National Strategy for Maritime Security and eight supporting implementation plans:

- **National Plan to Achieve Maritime Domain Awareness** lays the foundation for an effective understanding of anything associated with the Maritime Domain that could impact the security, safety, economy, or environment of the United States and identifying threats as early and as distant from our shores as possible.

- **Global Maritime Intelligence Integration Plan** uses existing capabilities to integrate all available intelligence regarding potential threats to U.S. interests in the Maritime Domain.

- **Maritime Operational Threat Response Plan** aims for coordinated U.S. Government response to threats against the United States and its interests in the Maritime Domain by establishing roles and responsibilities, which enable the government to respond quickly and decisively.

- **International Outreach and Coordination Strategy** provides a framework to coordinate all maritime security initiatives undertaken with foreign governments and international organizations, and solicits international support for enhanced maritime security.

- **Maritime Infrastructure Recovery Plan** recommends procedures and standards for the recovery of the maritime infrastructure following attack or similar disruption.

- **Maritime Transportation System Security Plan** responds to the President's call for recommendations to improve the national and international regulatory framework regarding the maritime domain.

- **Maritime Commerce Security Plan** establishes a comprehensive plan to secure the maritime supply chain.

- **Domestic Outreach Plan** engages non-Federal input to assist with the development and implementation of maritime security policies resulting from NSPD-41/HSPD-13.

Although these plans address different aspects of maritime security, they are mutually linked and reinforce each other. Together, the National Strategy for Maritime Security and its supporting plans represent a comprehensive national effort to enhance the security of the United States by preventing hostile or illegal acts within the Maritime Domain.

These plans do not alter existing constitutional or statutory authorities or responsibilities of the department and agency heads to carry out operational activities or to provide or receive information.

EXECUTIVE SUMMARY

The Marine Transportation System (MTS) generates nearly $750 billion of the U.S. Gross Domestic Product and handles 95% of all overseas trade.[1] The MTS makes it possible for goods from other countries to be delivered to our front door step. It enables the U.S. to project military presence across the globe, creates jobs that support local economies, and provides a source of recreation for all Americans. Fundamentally, the Nation's economic and military security are closely linked to the health and functionality of the MTS.[2]

As a Nation, we must do more to protect the MTS. We must prevent terrorist attacks which could destroy critical infrastructure and key assets in the maritime domain, and disrupt the MTS. That is why Maritime Transportation System Security is an essential component to the National Strategy for Maritime Security.

Improving security of the MTS while maintaining its functionality will not be an easy task. A complex system, the MTS is geographically diverse and composed of many types of assets, operations, and infrastructure that are operated and influenced by a diverse set of stakeholders, all of which play an important role in the system. In addition, the MTS is an open system which enables many users to use and benefit from it at minimal cost. The complexity and openness of the MTS make it efficient, however these characteristics also present many challenges to those trying to improve system security.

To overcome these challenges, the cooperation of all stakeholders is paramount and is central to improving security. Envision Maritime Transportation System Security as:

> *A systems-oriented security regime built upon layers of protection and defense-in-depth that effectively mitigates critical system security risks, while preserving the functionality and efficiency of the MTS. Understanding the most effective security risk management strategies involves cooperation and participation of both domestic and international stakeholders acting at strategic points in the system, the U.S. seeks to improve security through a cooperative and cohesive effort involving all stakeholders.*

This vision can further be thought of as a series of security nets providing layers of protection that are actualized by the following strategic recommendations. These recommendations will holistically improve security of the MTS and represent a significant step forward in protecting the most critical elements of the system while minimizing operational impacts. These strategic recommendations were developed in consultation with a wide spectrum of MTS stakeholders, including federal agencies, state and local governments, and industry representatives.

---

[1] American Association of Port Authorities. *America's Ports: Gateways to Global Trade.* Available: http://www.aapa-ports.org/industryinfo/americasports.htm , Last accessed: April 25, 2005
[2] Interagency Task Force on Coast Guard Roles and Missions. *A Coast Guard for the Twenty First Century: Report of the Interagency Task Force on U.S. Coast Guard Roles and Missions.* December 1999.

The Department of Homeland Security is responsible for overseeing the development and implementation of these recommendations:

- **Risk Management** - Improve Security management through the development and consistent application of risk assessment methodologies to prioritize and track the outcomes of security improvement efforts.
- **Security Information Management** - Develop an interagency security data management plan to improve the quality, transparency, sharing, and protection of critical security information among all appropriate MTS stakeholders, including federal, state, and local government agencies as well as MTS operators.
- **International & National Regulatory Framework** - Continually improve the international and national regulatory framework established by the International Ship and Port Facility Security Code (ISPS Code) and Maritime Transportation Security Act 2002 (MTSA 2002).
- **Stakeholder Responsibility & Coordination** - Create and manage a coordinated network of stakeholders who:
  (1) understand and accept their roles/responsibilities for ensuring maritime security; and,
  (2) are actively engaged in collaborative efforts to reduce security risks in the maritime domain.
- **Credentialing** - Develop the ability for U.S. authorities to identify with confidence:
  (1) individuals working aboard commercial vessels and operating recreational boats, foreign or domestic, in the U.S. Maritime Domain, and,
  (2) workers at land-based MTSA-regulated facilities and critical infrastructure components within the U.S. MTS.
- **Leverage Safety Frameworks** - Examine international, national, and industry transportation safety frameworks with respect to potential terrorist attack scenarios and determine if reasonable safety enhancements can significantly improve the inherent security of the MTS.
- **Security Technology** - Promote the development of technologies to address security gaps and improve the current Maritime Transportation System Security Network. Identify and support MTS changes needed to incorporate these technologies effectively into the security network.
- **Security Training** - Ensure that port and maritime personnel both domestically and internationally are properly trained in maritime security in accordance with their function within the MTS.

TABLE OF CONTENTS

I.   INTRODUCTION

The Marine Transportation System (MTS) is of tremendous value to the United States. The MTS:

- provides a global gateway to world markets for U.S. businesses and consumers;
- is a critical pathway for military mobilization;
- provides a network for domestic transportation of goods and passengers;
- creates jobs that support maritime operations (commercial and recreational);
- generates tax/tariff and operating fee revenues for federal, state, and local governments; and
- supports recreational use by the public.

The MTS generates nearly $750 billion of the U.S. Gross Domestic Product and handles 95% of all overseas trade yearly.[3] Fundamentally, the Nation's economic and military security are linked to the health and functionality of the MTS.[4] Without the MTS, a phenomenal amount of the goods and services so often taken for granted would vanish.

THE CHANGING FOCUS OF MARITIME SECURITY

Security in the Nation's seaports has been a concern and a shared responsibility from the start of the Nation. Responding to the urgent need for revenue following the American Revolutionary War, President George Washington signed the Tariff Act of July 4, 1789, which authorized the collection of duties on imported goods. Four weeks later, Congress established the United States Customs Service and ports of entry. Then in 1790, Congress formed the Revenue Cutter Service, under the direction of Alexander Hamilton, to enforce customs laws in the Maritime Domain.

Since those early beginnings, the U.S. Customs Service and the U.S. Coast Guard, joined by the U.S. Border Patrol, Immigration and Naturalization Service, and certain portions of the Department of Agriculture, have been charged with protecting the ports, waterways, and borders from criminal and/or terrorist acts. They continue to contribute to the security of the Nation by suppressing piracy, human smuggling, contraband smuggling, tariff evasion, illegal migration, illegal importation/exportation and other crimes within the ports.

Before 9/11, the Nation's primary maritime focus was on the safe and efficient use of America's waterways and prevention of criminal acts. The events of 9/11 changed the focus of maritime security. Fear of a terrorist attack or exploitation of the maritime domain by terrorists brought the focus on security to the forefront. As such, security improvements have responded to emerging threats in the maritime domain. Although the tariff collection and anticrime efforts

---

[3] American Association of Port Authorities. *America's Ports: Gateways to Global Trade.* Available: http://www.aapa-ports.org/industryinfo/americasports.htm , Last accessed: April 25, 2005
[4] Interagency Task Force on Coast Guard Roles and Missions. *A Coast Guard for the Twenty First Century: Report of the Interagency Task Force on U.S .Coast Guard Roles and Missions.* December 1999.

remain important functions for protecting the MTS, the primary focus has shifted to preventing a terrorist attack that would disrupt the critical free flow of commerce through the MTS. A balance must be achieved to provide the greatest protection possible in a free-flowing global trade environment.

Given the complexity of the MTS, it is apparent that this critical balance of security and commerce cannot be achieved without the cooperation and participation of both domestic and international stakeholders involved in the operation of the system. While all stakeholders want a secure MTS, none want to see reduced functionality or efficiency. How proposed and/or legislated security measures will impact the operational capabilities of the MTS is foremost in their minds. However, just as important but often not as tangible is how those security measures help reduce risk in the MTS. Stakeholder understanding of how public and private contributions will positively impact the resiliency and functionality of the MTS will alleviate concerns and bolster a resolve to contribute.

A SYSTEMS VIEW

The MTS is a complex system with many types of assets, operations, and infrastructure as well as a widely diverse set of stakeholders. From a systems perspective, the MTS is a **network** of maritime operations that interface with shoreside operations at intermodal connections as part of overall global supply chains or domestic commercial operations. The various maritime operations within the MTS operating network have **components** that include vessels, port facilities, waterways and waterway infrastructure, intermodal connections, and users. These components share **critical interfaces** with each other and with overarching **information systems** such as maritime commerce systems and Maritime Domain Awareness (MDA) systems. Refer to Appendix C for a graphical representation of the systems view.

Improving security of the MTS as a system of systems focuses on four primary elements:

- **Component Security.** MTS component security ensures that the individual physical components (e.g., vessels, vehicles, facilities, infrastructure items, and cargo) have measures in place to prevent exploitation and to protect against attack.
- **Interface Security.** MTS interface security addresses the potential for corruption between modes of transportation and at key interactions between MTS components.
- **Information Security.** MTS information security ensures that key data systems (1) are not corrupted or exploited by terrorists, and (2) are continually available to support maritime operations (including security management functions).
- **Network Security.** Network security is the "big picture view" that focuses on enhancing security through the overarching systems that drive the MTS as a whole.

Understanding of the MTS as a system of systems helps in the development of strategic efforts to fulfill the vision to improve Maritime Transportation System Security.

VISION FOR MARITIME TRANSPORTATION SYSTEM SECURITY

A systems-oriented security regime built upon layers of protection and defense-in-depth that effectively mitigates critical system security risks, while preserving the functionality and efficiency of the MTS. Understanding the most effective security risk management strategies involves cooperation and participation of both domestic and international stakeholders acting at strategic points in the system, the U.S. seeks to improve security through a cooperative and cohesive effort involving all stakeholders.

This vision for Maritime Transportation System Security can best be expressed as a series of security nets that provide layers of protection necessary to effectively manage security risks. Figure 3.1 illustrates the concept of these security nets for key elements of the MTS.

Figure 3.1 Concept for Security Net the MTS

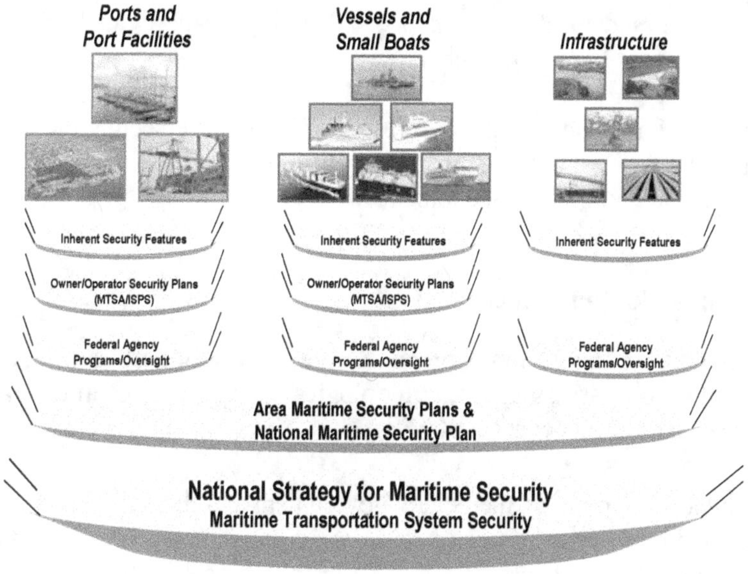

II. Strategic Recommendations

Maritime Transportation System Security is an essential component to the National Strategy for Maritime Security. As a Nation we must do more to prevent terrorist attacks in the maritime domain, and protect critical infrastructure and key assets which are part of the MTS. Enclosed are recommendations to improve the national and international regulatory framework for all private and commercial operations in the maritime domain. To ensure a holistic solution, these recommendations also address land-based infrastructure and intermodal connections that are vital for moving goods and people across the United States.

Stakeholder participation in security of the MTS is essential to keeping America out of harm's way. As a result and as part of the development of these recommendations, extensive outreach was conducted to over 2,700 individuals representing over four (4) million private-sector organizations and state and local governments. Their input was crucial to developing sound recommendations for security improvements.

The Department of Homeland Security is responsible for overseeing the development and implementation of the following recommendations to improve Maritime Transportation System Security in coordination with MTS stakeholders.

Recommendation: Risk Management

Improve security management through the development and consistent application of risk assessment methodologies to prioritize and track the outcomes of security improvement efforts.

Since 9/11, much has been done by the federal government and the various stakeholders to make the MTS more secure by deterring terrorists, decreasing the vulnerability of assets, and putting in place measures to mitigate the consequences of a terrorist attack. Central to these efforts, risk management principles have provided a framework for stakeholders to characterize risk, prioritize efforts/resources, and achieve a balance between system security and functionality. We must continue to build upon this framework and knowledge base by developing risk assessment methodologies and consistently applying them across all agencies.

We must transition to the use of a common risk framework, which will allow the results of a risk analysis done by owners and operators, or sector specific agencies, to be comparable and useful for supporting security related decisions. This framework must be built on a central risk management system which contains a comprehensive set of threat, vulnerability, and consequence data. This system will guide our decisions, and also help to:

- Ensure sufficient public and private resources are focused on the practical mitigation of the most serious threats in (and through) the maritime domain.

- Promote a continuous awareness of ever-changing maritime domain security risks at the international, national, regional, and local levels so that all key stakeholders can quickly react to changing threat environments in a coordinated way.
- Enact necessary changes in regulatory frameworks and policies to provide substantial impacts on key risks without overly burdening operations in the MTS.
- Provide a compelling, technically defensible basis for the key elements of the maritime security policy, including benefit (risk reduction) versus cost evaluations of strategy options.
- Establish a common focal point on important risks and a decision-making discipline that helps produce a fully coordinated U.S. government effort that protects U.S. interests in the MTS.

For this risk framework to flourish and succeed, we must provide all agencies with the proper training and tools. These will not only help users to understand the risks and risk assessment methodologies, but also provide them with the knowledge to communicate the risks to all stakeholders.

DHS shall consider the following guidelines for detailed implementation of this recommendation.

- Establish a Maritime Domain Security Risk Information Management System to provide a strategic view of the diverse risks at the national and local levels based on best available interagency information.
- Develop a consistent Risk Assessment Methodology for collecting and developing risk data.
- Provide tools and training for using risk assessment data at all levels of the MTS.
- Develop models to reduce the uncertainty surrounding threat, vulnerability and consequence.

Recommendation: Security Information Management

Develop an interagency security data management plan to improve the quality, transparency, sharing, and protection of critical security information among all appropriate MTS stakeholders, including federal, state, and local government agencies as well as MTS operators.

Multiple agencies and operators make up the security nets protecting the MTS. To serve their roles in security effectively, stakeholders need critical information that often is distributed among several databases/sources across multiple agencies. Failing to have reliable transparent information readily accessible will hinder security efforts to detect, interdict, respond to, and recover from possible terrorist attacks. Layers of protection and defense-in-depth against all of the high-risk scenarios are only effective if pertinent information can pass through the security management system's critical interfaces for stakeholders to use. Similar to selected findings of the 9/11 Commission, this recommendation recognizes current gaps in sharing intelligence, strategic plans, and operational data among federal agencies. These gaps are further compounded for state/local government agencies and private entities because of the classified or sensitive nature of much of the information.

A proper balance between information transparency/sharing and information security must be achieved. Allowing information to fall into the wrong hands will enable terrorists to exploit the security network. And, if access to information systems is not secure, terrorists will be able to create "covers" to hide movement of terrorists and materials for performing terrorist acts.

Government agencies continue to share information that facilitates screening capabilities and optimizes safe and effective law enforcement actions. Nevertheless, opportunity remains to improve efficiencies and build upon existing relationships.

DHS shall consider the following guidelines for detailed implementation of this recommendation.

- Seek additional authority to compel reporting of critical security information or to gain access to the information in other ways.
- Implement systems necessary to collect/use/share the additional data that will be collected.
- Engage, through the U.S. Coast Guard, the National Maritime Security Advisory Committee to identify and recommend approaches for closing recognized security gaps.
- Ensure appropriate documentation practices are implemented for all commercial and private vessels so that enforcement authorities will have an enhanced capability to identify the true owners of vessels.
- Pursue tighter controls concerning transparency of vessel ownership and operations internationally.
- Leverage an increased security presence by promoting interagency operations and Memorandums of Agreement / Memorandums of Understanding (MOAs/MOUs) that specifically address information-sharing needs among federal agencies as well as sharing with state/local agencies and applicable international agencies.
- Form and use a standing interagency working group to (1) identify data compatibility and access barriers for key maritime security data among the agencies and (2) ensure ongoing compatibility as new systems come online.
- Continue implementation of systems such as the Homeland Security Information Network (HSIN) to create an intelligence network that will enhance MDA with data links and portals for two-way information sharing with federal, state, and local agencies as well as private sector/commercial operators.
- Employ an overall, interagency cybersecurity framework that ensures the most appropriate and cost-effective cybersecurity technologies are in place to protect classified or sensitive security data.
- Use industry outreach to help commercial operators understand what private information could be exploited by terrorists and what cybersecurity controls are appropriate for protecting the information.

Recommendation: International & National Regulatory Framework

Continually improve the international and national regulatory framework established by the ISPS Code and MTSA 2002.

The ISPS Code and MTSA 2002 were landmark achievements within the maritime community and have gone far to enhance maritime security around the world. Continued improvements to this framework will solidify the foundation of global maritime security. By balancing trade and the flow of goods and services while implementing new measures to improve security, the U.S. will continue to preserve the functionality of the MTS.

DHS shall consider the following guidelines for detailed implementation of this recommendation.

- Encourage the International Maritime Organization (IMO) to include the maritime security measures adopted in the ISPS Code within the framework of the Voluntary IMO Member State Audit Scheme.
- Coordinate with other Member States at the IMO to develop a permanent forum on maritime security standards.
- Pursue the development of performance-oriented international standards for maritime security. Continue to work with the IMO and World Customs Organization to encourage and assist in the development of recommendations on performance-oriented international security standards.
- Update the MTSA 2002 regulations.
- Pursue international efforts to promote flag state accountability and increase vessel ownership transparency.

Recommendation: Stakeholder Responsibility & Coordination

Create and manage a coordinated network of stakeholders who:
(1) understand and accept their roles/responsibilities for ensuring maritime security; and,
(2) are actively engaged in collaborative efforts to reduce security risks in the Maritime Domain.

The National Strategy for Maritime Security is based on providing layers of protection against high-risk issues. Many different agencies (federal, state, and local) as well as commercial operators, maritime organizations, and the recreational boating community play key roles in providing these layers of protection. No one agency can (or should) directly address all of the security risks associated with the MTS. The diversity of risk reduction activities and distributed roles/responsibilities provide defense-in-depth, while (1) minimizing the potential for single-point organizational failures to result in catastrophic consequences and (2) leveraging the resources of a vast global network of stakeholders for improving maritime security. Significant progress has been made in stakeholder coordination, including:

- Area Maritime Security Committees
- National Maritime Security Advisory Committee
- Security discussions among the Coast Guard's various industry safety advisory committees
- Federal interagency working groups on specific topics (e.g., ferry security)
- Government-industry partnerships such as Customs-Trade Partnership against Terrorism (C-TPAT), Operation Safe Commerce, America's Waterway Watch, Information Sharing and Analysis Centers, etc.
- International maritime security initiatives through IMO (e.g., the ISPS Code)

Although many new initiatives are being implemented in the Maritime Domain to combat the most significant threats/risks, coordination of planning/implementation among various governments, agencies, and maritime operating communities remains elusive. Opportunities for improvement exist, especially in the areas of (1) defining and communicating responsibilities to stakeholders and (2) facilitating collaborative continuous improvement of security management strategies with stakeholders.

The federal government is best positioned and has the responsibility to implement this recommendation. Domestically, we must clearly define expectations for all of the stakeholders. We must hold them accountable for fulfilling their roles/responsibilities, and we must provide incentives for excellent security management performance and measured penalties for inadequate performance. Internationally, we must communicate expectations to other governments and the international maritime community by providing appropriate incentives/penalties based on performance wherever possible. Finally, we must engage domestic and international stakeholders/partners on an ongoing basis with the challenging work of optimizing security, safety, and protection of the maritime domain with minimal impacts on global trade and recreational uses of our waterways.

DHS shall consider the following guidelines for detailed implementation of this recommendation.

- Establish an interdepartmental committee to focus on security coordination for the MTS.
- Enter into formal MOAs/MOUs with states for domestic maritime security coordination.
- Encourage, through the Department of State, foreign governments to conform to internationally accepted standards for maritime security and to meaningfully commit to sustained improvements in maritime security performance.
- Review membership of the Area Maritime Security Committees to ensure all appropriate stakeholders are represented.
- Develop communication vehicles that can link appropriate stakeholders for information sharing during normal and threat response/recovery modes.
- Ensure appropriate stakeholders have access to information at a level consistent with applicable regulations.

- Establish and maintain a Web-based secure portal with active notification systems for the maritime community.
- Establish a framework or process where industry, state and local governments, and federal government agencies can come together and interact during normal operations to
  - equip local stakeholders with real-time information awareness;
  - engage broader groups of local stakeholders in security; and
  - extend participation in security planning to the working level, not just at the Area Maritime Security Committee level.
- Ensure primary stakeholders, Department of Defense (through the Army Corps of Engineers), the Department of Transportation, and local transportation entities, are included in maritime infrastructure development projects.

Recommendation: Credentialing

Develop the ability of the U.S. to identify:

(1) individuals working aboard commercial vessels and operating recreational boats, foreign or domestic, in the U.S. Maritime Domain; and

(2) workers at land-based MTSA-regulated facilities and critical infrastructure components within the U.S. MTS.

The objective of the U.S. is to identify individuals working in, operating on, or using the U.S. MTS. Effective access control and reliable identification of persons are important layers of protection for improving security in the Maritime Domain. Appropriate security vetting and identity verification for credentials for the various types of people working and operating in the Maritime Domain are critical for access control and for governmental authorities to identify persons warranting further evaluation. Currently, not all individuals working in the Maritime Domain are credibly identified and vetted.

DHS shall consider the following guidelines for detailed implementation of this recommendation.

- Ensure all transportation workers at MTSA-regulated land-based facilities and all workers on U.S. flag vessels not required to have a Coast Guard issued credential, have a Transportation Worker Identification Card (TWIC).
- Require licensed officers, and navigating and engineering crewmembers aboard U.S. flag commercial vessels to undergo security screening. Other workers who are not required to have a Coast Guard issued credential should undergo security screening and be required to carry a TWIC.
- Align the Merchant Mariners Document (MMD) and the TWIC so the MMD satisfies all TWIC requirements for MTS access.

- Increase deployment of US-VISIT technology.
- Require recreational boaters to carry a state-issued form of personal identification.

Recommendation: Leverage Safety Frameworks

> **Examine international, national, and industry transportation safety frameworks with respect to potential terrorist attack scenarios and determine if reasonable safety enhancements can significantly improve the inherent security of the MTS.**

International, national, and industry frameworks regarding licensing, safety equipment, communications, and other critical systems aboard vessels and within the MTS have focused on preventing marine accidents (e.g., flooding due to an unintentional grounding, fire or explosion due to a machinery malfunction, and collision avoidance by traffic separation schemes or regulated navigational areas) or managing the risks associated with marine accidents. These frameworks improve the physical safety of MTS components and have the added benefit of enhancing the physical security of the component. While the type of damage in a marine accident and the type of damage from a terrorist attack may be similar, the degree of damage and the rapid deterioration of conditions associated with some terrorist attacks may exceed the ability of current safety measures to mitigate consequences. As such, we must examine transportation safety frameworks to determine if reasonable safety enhancements can significantly improve the inherent security of the MTS.

Following the attacks in the United States on September 11, 2001, and amidst pressure from the international community to address the vulnerabilities of the MTS to a terrorist attack, the IMO has recognized that safety and security are intertwined. Hence, they developed the ISPS Code. The ISPS Code is a comprehensive set of requirements to enhance the security of ships and port facilities, which was implemented as an amendment to International Convention for the Safety of Life at Sea, 1974 (SOLAS). The ISPS Code reduces the vulnerability of vessels and facilities through requirements that improve organic security and access controls. However, the ISPS Code does not address the physical vulnerability of vessels that stems from their design and survivability characteristics, nor does it address lifesaving equipment, which may help to mitigate the consequences of an attack. These safety traits, often referred to as "target hardness" in the security risk management context, provide vessels with layers of safety protection. These same layers can also enhance the layers of security protection. By decreasing the physical vulnerability of vessels through new design criteria or improved training of first responders/crewmembers, and mitigating the consequences of an attack through improved requirements for lifesaving, communications, and critical systems, it may be possible to achieve an overall reduction in risk to vessels.

Similarly, safety regulations for other modes of transportation can also help reduce security risks. These regulations can affect security risks aboard vessels, on shore facilities, at intermodal connections, and where other transportation modes interact with MTS infrastructure.

Given recent intelligence regarding the threats to maritime assets and the attractiveness of these assets to terrorist organizations, it would be prudent to review transportation safety regulations to determine if reasonable changes could be made that enhance security.

DHS shall consider the following guidelines for detailed implementation of this recommendation.

- Work with international, national, and industry regulatory bodies that develop transportation safety regulations to consider whether current regulations need to be revised to manage the risks associated with a terrorist attack.
- Build on existing tools already in place for safety and waterways management such as Vessel Traffic Systems to enhance security.

Recommendation: Security Technology

Promote the development of technologies to address security gaps and improve the current Maritime Transportation System Security Network. Identify and support MTS changes needed to incorporate these technologies effectively into the security network.

Technology plays a significant role in a comprehensive security network. Nonlethal devices for stopping vessels, boat barriers, and underwater security methods are just a few examples of technology developed to address security needs. Efforts such as the Advanced Container Security Device, Operation Safe Commerce, and the development of Non-Intrusive Inspection and "smart box" technology are perfect examples of technology at work to secure the MTS. As an added benefit, much of the information or technology deployed for security can also be used to expedite and facilitate management of the MTS.

A number of gaps were identified in the Maritime Transportation System Security Network that could be adequately addressed with technology. The proper application of existing technologies or the development of new technologies can address security issues such as:

- Terrorist infiltration via cargo containers
- Small boat terrorist attack
- Detection of radiological, nuclear, chemical and biological terrorist weapons on international vessels (passenger and cargo)
- Response capability to deal with Chemical, Biological, Radiological, Nuclear, and High-Yield Explosive (CBRNE) terrorist events on a vessel
- Underwater detection of terrorist activity
- Rapid response to a terrorist event on a ship or in a port

The federal government should encourage the use of technology for improving maritime security and remain a central figure in developing relevant technology. DHS shall consider the following guidelines for detailed implementation of this recommendation.

- Promote policies to encourage the rapid deployment of security technologies into the MTS.

- Develop technology specification guides for application of technology to various security needs.
- Incorporate "lessons learned" from field applications into future security technology development and specification.
- Develop security technology solutions that are adaptable to the existing MTS framework.

Recommendation: Security Training

Ensure that port and maritime personnel both domestically and internationally are properly trained in maritime security in accordance with their function within the MTS.

The U.S. Congress, through MTSA 2002, and the IMO, through the ISPS Code, explicitly recognized the critical importance of properly trained personnel in the enhancement of maritime security. To support this effort the U.S. has created a national system of certification and course approval for the training of U.S. maritime security personnel, which includes federal, state, and local officials as well as private sector personnel. In addition, the U.S. is currently offering security training as part of its international antiterrorism programs. While there has been much progress in this area, more comprehensive and sustained efforts both domestically and internationally are needed to engage all stakeholders and leverage the eyes and ears of all MTS workers.

Domestically and internationally, there is a need to increase the training capacity of carriers and facilities that lack the resources to provide all workers with recurring security training. This training will not only help personnel to recognize security vulnerabilities, it will also arm them with the knowledge to address and resolve them. Beyond the current security training requirements, a more comprehensive training program needs to address other MTS workers who are not typically part of current security teams. By engaging all stakeholders through security training, we can make it more difficult for terrorists to exploit the vulnerabilities of vessels, facilities, and infrastructure of the MTS.

DHS shall consider the following guidelines for detailed implementation of this recommendation:

- Expand education and security training for maritime transportation workers at U.S. shore facilities.
- Expand security training for developing countries.
- Include risk management principles in maritime security training.
- Expand the Department of Energy Megaports Initiative.

APPENDIX A: ACRONYMS AND TERMS

Acronym	Definition
CBRNE	Chemical, Biological, Radiological, Nuclear, and High-Yield Explosive
C-TPAT	Customs-Trade Partnership against Terrorism
DHS	Department of Homeland Security
HSIN	Homeland Security Information Network
HSPD	Homeland Security Presidential Directive
IMO	International Maritime Organization
ISPS Code	International Ship and Port Facility Security Code
MDA	Maritime Domain Awareness
MMD	Merchant Mariner Document
MOA	Memorandum of Agreement
MOU	Memorandum of Understanding
MTS	Marine Transportation System
MTSA 2002	Maritime Transportation Security Act of 2002
NSMS	National Strategy for Maritime Security
NSPD	National Security Presidential Directive
SOLAS	International Convention for the Safety of Life at Sea, 1974
TWIC	Transportation Workers Identification Credential
U.S.	United States

APPENDIX B: ALIGNMENT WITH THE NATIONAL STRATEGY

The recommendations for improving Maritime Transportation System Security are just one of many efforts under the National Strategy for Maritime Security. Table 3.1 highlights the alignment of these recommendations with the objectives and elements of the National Strategy.

Table B.1 Alignment of Maritime Transportation System Security Recommendations with the National Strategy for Maritime Security

National Strategy (Objectives & Elements)	Related?	Degree of Coverage by the Security Recommendations	Related Recommendations
Objectives			
Prevent Terrorist Attacks and Criminal Acts	✓	During the development of the recommendations, a wide range of possible terrorist attacks addressed in existing security risk assessments were considered. The recommendations focus on major Security gaps associated with the highest risk issues, specifically addressing whether the gaps existed in threat reduction, vulnerability reduction, and/or consequence management.	All
Protect Maritime – related Population Centers and Infrastructure	✓	The recommendations consider the international and national regulatory framework for maritime security, which includes updates to the ISPS Code and MTSA 2002.	All
Minimize Damage and Expedite Recovery	✓	Many recommendations address preparedness issues as part of discussions of possible consequence management gaps. The "leveraging safety regulations" recommendation focuses on measures to minimize the damage associated with a terrorist attack.	• Risk Management • Security Information Management • International & National Regulatory Framework • Stakeholder Responsibility/ Coordination • Leveraging Safety Equipment/ Frameworks • Security Technology • Security Training
Safeguard the Oceans and Its Resources	✓	The previous risk assessments reviewed during the development of the recommendations considered a wide range of consequences that terrorist acts might have on the Maritime Domain (safety/health, economic, environmental, military operation impacts, etc.).	All

Table B.1 Alignment of Maritime Transportation System Security Recommendations with the National Strategy for Maritime Security (continued)

National Strategy (Objectives & Elements)	Related?	Degree of Coverage by the Security Recommendations	Related Recommendations
Elements			
Create International Security Frameworks	✓	The recommendations address updates to both domestic and international security frameworks including gaps in regulatory frameworks.	• International & National Regulatory Framework • Stakeholder Responsibility/ Coordination
Maximize Domain Awareness	✓	The recommendations address MDA by underscoring the importance of information management and stakeholder coordination.	• Security Information Management • Stakeholder Responsibility/ Coordination • Security Technology
Embed Security Into Commercial Practices	✓	The recommendations address updates to domestic and international security frameworks as well as existing safety regulations to embed security into commercial practices.	• International & National Regulatory Framework • Leveraging Safety Equipment/ Frameworks
Deploy Layered Security	✓	Layer of protection and defense-in-depth concepts are fundamental to the recommendations.	• Stakeholder Responsibility/ Coordination • Credentialing • Security Training
Assure MTS Continuity	✓	Assuring MTS continuity was a fundamental concept in developing the recommendations. Specifically, the risk management recommendation addresses interruption of MTS continuity as a consequence of terrorist attacks.	• Risk Management • Stakeholder Responsibility/ Coordination

APPENDIX C: A SYSTEMS VIEW OF THE MTS

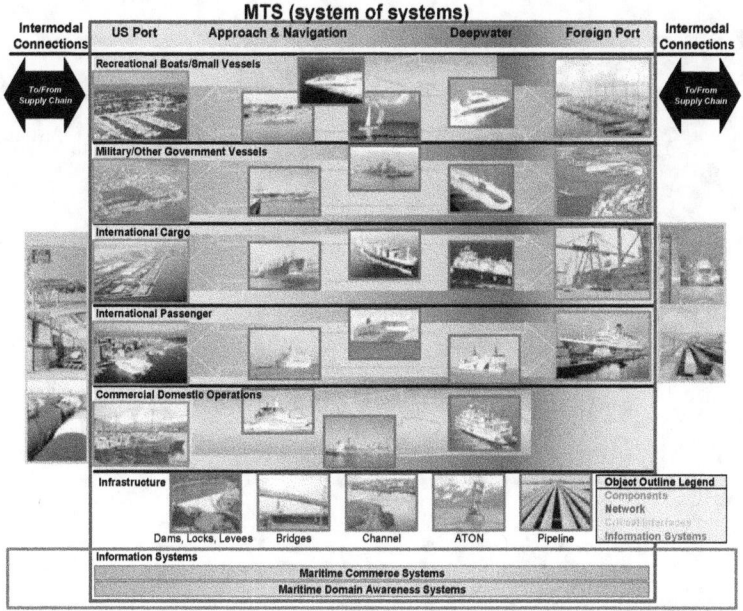

Figure C.1 A Systems View of the MTS

www.ingramcontent.com/pod-product-compliance
Lightning Source LLC
Chambersburg PA
CBHW080403290526

45790CB00009BA/3675